At David C Cook, we equip the local church around
the corner and around the globe to make disciples.
Come see how we are working together—go to
www.davidccook.org. Thank you!

transforming lives together

Yes, No, & Maybe

STUDY GUIDE

STUDY GUIDE
SIX SESSIONS

Yes, No, & Maybe

Living with the God of Immeasurably More

Wendy Pope

DAVID C COOK

transforming lives together

YES, NO, AND MAYBE STUDY GUIDE
Published by David C Cook
4050 Lee Vance Drive
Colorado Springs, CO 80918 U.S.A.

Integrity Music Limited, a Division of David C Cook
Eastbourne, East Sussex BN23 6NT, England

The graphic circle C logo is a registered trademark of David C Cook.

The website addresses recommended throughout this book are offered as a
resource to you. These websites are not intended in any way to be or imply an
endorsement on the part of David C Cook, nor do we vouch for their content.

Details in some stories have been changed to protect
the identities of the persons involved.

Bible credits are listed at the back of this book.
The author has added italics to Scripture quotations for emphasis.

ISBN 978-0-8307-7587-3
eISBN 978-0-8307-7625-2

The Team: Wendi Lord, Nick Lee, Laura Derico, Susan Murdock
Cover Design: Amy Konyndyk
Cover Photo: Getty Images

Printed in the United States of America
First Edition 2018

1 2 3 4 5 6 7 8 9 10

080618

Related titles:

*Yes, No, and Maybe: Living with the
God of Immeasurably More*

Yes, No, and Maybe Video Series

Available now!

Contents

Welcome

Welcome to the *Yes, No, and Maybe Study Guide.* One of my favorite things is to meet and spend time with God's girls. Warmth fills my entire body when I sit and talk about Jesus with other women. There's nothing quite like Holy Spirit synergy. Don't you agree?

I'm excited to invite you to have Bible study with me. In each of the accompanying video sessions (available separately), I'll meet with you from the beautiful chapel on the campus of my church. You can picture what the chapel looks like. Huge heavy wooden doors. Stained glass windows. A center aisle, with pews lined up neatly on both sides. A slight echo, perfect for hymns to fill the air.

Just thinking about our meeting together makes me all giddy inside. We get to spend six sessions together! Oh, how I wish I could be in the room with you, sitting around the table, hearing the rustling of the pages of your Bibles, or seeing the glow of screens as you scroll through your Bible apps. Studying the Bible is fun, but it's so exciting to study God's Word with friends. Thank you for allowing me to be part of your group.

When I wrote this Bible study, I had you in mind. Life is busy, schedules are crazy, work and family demands are at an all-time high. Now, more than ever, we need to be in the Word of God, yet there seems to be less time to do so. The *Yes, No, and Maybe Study Guide* will not add to your weekly stresses. It will be a soft and safe place to land for loving encouragement. I like to call it a guilt-free Bible study.

We often allow incomplete homework to prevent us from returning to Bible study. Then we feel guilty because we didn't finish the study, and as a result, we remain stagnant in our spiritual growth. This is exactly where Satan wants us to be. I want the *Yes, No, and Maybe* (YNM) experience to expand your knowledge of the Word, generate excitement in your heart to study the Bible, and help you grow in Christian fellowship with your sisters in Christ. And this won't happen if you aren't in class because you didn't finish your homework. So, in this study we don't have any homework or required* outside reading. (I think I hear shouting—"Woo hoo!") You're welcome.

The study will work like this: grab your guide and your Bible (or favorite device loaded with your favorite Bible app) and meet with your group. You can watch a short video teaching, and then work through the Bible study questions together. It's that simple.

And all God's girls said, "AMEN and let's begin!" I'll meet you in the chapel.

Serving Him until I see Him,
Wendy

P. S. And for my sisters who like to have a little study during the week, I have included something for you. At the close of each lesson there is a section called On Your Own ... If You Want To. This is a short, non-mandatory assignment. It's not your ticket to get back in class next week. It's simply optional material to enhance your study ... if you want to.

*This study guide is the companion to my book *Yes, No, and Maybe: Living with the God of Immeasurably More*. Reading the *Yes, No, and Maybe* book is not required or necessary to complete the Bible study. However, in each session we have noted the chapters that go with that teaching (look for the YNM Reading heading), so you can read those chapters along with your study material, which will provide you with a richer experience—full of stories and more lessons I've learned through my life with the God of immeasurably more.

Tips for Leading

As a Bible study leader, I understand the commitment it takes to shepherd a small group. It is my honor to pray for those of you who are leading as you accompany your wonderful group on their *Yes, No, and Maybe* adventure. Whether you are facilitating just one session, or leading a whole group through all the sessions, the time and thought and prayer you give to your group is so valuable. I hope you find this guide helpful as you lead.

Besides this guide, these resources are available:

- *Yes, No, and Maybe: Living with the God of Immeasurably More* (available as a printed book or as an ebook)

- *Yes, No, and Maybe Video Series* (available as a DVD or as a downloadable file)

Let's have a look at what happens in each session. As you begin the study with your group, notice that each session is anchored by a Key Verse. I suggest you pray together as you start, then ask the Connect Question to get people talking. Next, you can watch the video teaching segment. A Video Listening Guide is provided for each session to help people follow along and note significant concepts. Then you and your group will work through the rest of the study together, learning about how our yes cultivates trust, no invites revelation, and maybe welcomes freedom. We'll also unpack some of the teachings of Paul, who is responsible for much of what we read in our New Testament. Finally, the On Your Own … If You Want To section gives ideas and questions for further study that participants can do on their own time, if they so desire—and with no pressure!

It is my privilege to open the Holy Scriptures with you, and to partner with you as you take the first steps on your very own Yes, No, and Maybe adventure. Let's get moving!

BEFORE YOUR FIRST MEETING

- Secure a meeting place with the appropriate equipment to view the video.
- Enlist other small group leaders, as needed.
- Promote the time, place, and topic of the Bible study.
- Determine childcare provision.
- Pray for the participants and leaders.

- Create a list of counselors and counseling centers. Bring it to class each week. Bible study has the potential to unearth hidden hurts that may need professional attention.

TIME MANAGEMENT

Time is a valuable commodity. Your class members are sacrificing something to be part of this Bible study. It's essential to respect their time. Holding to the schedule is more than just watching the clock.

As the facilitator, you might press play and stop for the video, but you will also figuratively press play and stop for discussion. Your group may include a Chatty Cathy, a Know-It-All Nancy, and a Problem-Solver Patty. Cathy likes to talk—a lot! Nancy is an expert on virtually every topic, and Patty wants to resolve everyone's issues. The best way to address these three personalities is to keep moving through the study questions, even if it means politely bringing responses to a close by saying, "Thank you, Cathy. Anyone else have thoughts?" or "Great insight, Patty. Let's move on to the next question." If some people habitually monopolize the group discussion, it might be helpful to have a private talk with those individuals outside of your group time.

You may have a group full of Silent Sues. Sue may have a lot to say, but she is intimidated to speak out. Or maybe Sue is a new student of the Word and fears giving the wrong answer. The Connect Questions are designed to help the Silent Sues in your group by giving them questions they know how to answer. Remember, silence is not a bad thing. Don't be afraid of it. Pauses are good and give your group time to process what God is teaching them.

PRAYER TIME

Prayer is how we communicate with God and definitely should be included in the Bible study sessions. We suggest you start and end each group time in prayer. Of course, not everyone likes to pray aloud. As the leader, you can be the designated pray-er, or you can enlist a few volunteers. Through the power of the Holy Spirit, God uses our prayers for each other to connect our hearts to Him, as well as to one another. Here are a few suggestions for receiving prayer requests:

- Adjust your schedule by 15 minutes at the end or the beginning to accept prayer requests.
- Individuals can write their requests on a whiteboard. At the end of class, ask for volunteers to commit to pray for requests during the week.
- Participants can write their requests on pieces of paper and place the papers in a basket. Instruct the class, "If you leave a request, take a request."

BEFORE EACH SESSION

- Arrive early to pray for the participants.
- Arrange chairs and tables.

- Load and cue up the video.
- Prepare to receive prayer requests. (See Prayer Time.)
- Write the Connect Question on the board, if you have one.
- Welcome the group members as they arrive, calling each person by name.

SUGGESTED SCHEDULES

As you learn the needs of your participants, choose a format that works for you.

1-Hour Class

10 min.: Prayer and welcome.

15–20 min.: Video teaching session and Video Listening Guide.

30 min.: Participants use their Bibles and work in a small group to answer the study questions. As the leader, make yourself available to share the answers to the questions.

1.5-Hour Class

10 min.: Prayer and welcome.

15–20 min.: Video teaching session and Video Listening Guide.

45 min.: Participants use their Bibles and work in a small group to answer the study questions.

15 min.: Use the remaining minutes of class to discuss the answers to the questions together as a group.

AFTER EACH SESSION

- Put the video and video equipment away.
- Reset tables and chairs, as needed.
- Erase the whiteboard. (To ensure confidentiality, don't leave prayer requests on the board.)
- Encourage your participants throughout the days following the session: use email or text to send them scriptures and uplifting quotes from the study.

Yes to God: What Does Yes Mean?

PRAYER

Let someone pray for the beginning of your *Yes, No, and Maybe* adventure together.

CONNECT QUESTION

What was one request you were happy to say "yes" to recently?

KEY VERSE

"You have been set free from sin and have become slaves to righteousness" (Rom. 6:18).

BIBLE READING

Romans 6:16–18

YNM READING

Introduction and chapter 1

VIDEO LISTENING GUIDE

Our experience with the immeasurably more God starts with a yes from the heart.

Yes means _____ to God, rather than to our own wants and wishes.

We say yes to His _____, rather than leaning on our own thoughts, education, and intellect.

We say yes to His _____ _____, rather than our own sinful nature.

Life with the God of immeasurably more starts when we allow yes to cultivate trust and no to invite revelation, so maybe can welcome freedom.

SESSION 1 NOTES

SESSION 1 DISCUSSION

A few years ago, my son got caught up in the *Walking Dead* craze. The television show is based on a comic book series that tells the story of life after a zombie apocalypse. The survivors interact with zombies—will-less and speechless human characters who have died and been supernaturally reanimated—while trying to find a safe and secure place to live. It's a little too gruesome for my taste, but to a teenage boy it screams "Cool."

But I found myself wondering, could it be we have more in common with the walking dead than we think?

While it's not a perfect analogy, before Christ, all of us—me, you, and even people in the Bible, like Saul—were the walking dead. We were spiritually dead. *Spiritually dead* means being separated from God by sin. We walked around among the living, unable to speak or understand matters of the Spirit, looking for a safe and secure place to be. The divide between God and the human race caused by sin was closed by the grace of God through the sacrificial death of His Son, Jesus. Now, those who trust Jesus as their Savior are truly alive, with the indwelling of the Holy Spirit, walking in the security of our heavenly home, able to speak and understand spiritual matters. However, we, much like the early believers, live with the constant threat of an enemy—Satan—who hates us and God.

Saul (later called Paul) had hate in his heart and aimed to kill Christians near and far. He was a rising leader among the Jews, and he saw Christianity as a threat to Judaism. We're introduced to him as a man who was "breathing out murderous threats against the Lord's disciples" (Acts 9:1). This ruthless persecutor set out on another mission of murder, having no idea that *he* was a dead man walking. That is, until Jesus stepped onto the scene.

Only a radical encounter with God could change a man who reviled Christianity into a man who felt like this: "For, as I have often told you before and now tell you again *even with tears*, many live as enemies of the cross of Christ" (Phil. 3:18). Such a drastic change in someone's heart and trajectory of life can only be attributed to salvation. Salvation is a one-time act that compels us into a lifetime of action. Thankfully, we have God to help us every step of the way.

1. Spend a moment reflecting on a time when you became aware of a desire to take a step of faith. For those of you who have already accepted Christ as your Savior, think about the day of your salvation. Where were you and who was there?

The experience of salvation is the beginning of a lifetime adventure with the creator of the universe through the person of the Holy Spirit. Jesus saved us, and the Holy Spirit seeks to sanctify us. *Sanctify* is a church word you may or may not have heard before. *Sanctify* means "to be set apart or made holy." Simply put, we can define *sanctification* as the state in which we become like Christ, to be used by Christ, for the glory of Christ. On our Damascus Road experience—like Paul's—Jesus gives us new life. Then, in this life, His Spirit helps us to override our sinful nature and overcome our past, so we can be holy as He is holy.

OVERRIDING OUR SINFUL NATURE

Read Ephesians 2:1–9. Keep your Bible open to Ephesians 2.

2. What does verse 1 say you were? What does verse 5 say God made us?

Compare those two words: *dead* and *alive*. It makes sense that the word *dead* in the Greek would mean "what lacks life," but take a look at the word *alive*. The word *alive* is part of a compound Greek expression that means "made us alive together." The word that translates as this phrase is made up of two root words: *sýn* (soon), which means "joined close-together in tight identification,"[1] and *zōopoiéō* (dzo-op-oy-eh'-o), which "is particularly used of God *infusing His life in the believer.*"[2] You can't get more opposite than that! We were the walking dead, but now we are infused with Christ. Wowsers! Don't you just love studying God's Word?

Adam's sin in the Garden separating us from God = dead. Jesus's sacrifice on the cross opening the door for unity with God = alive. Salvation is the free gift of God that rescues us from the power of sin. It takes us from death to life, old to new, what *was* to what *will be*. Such good news seems too good to be true, doesn't it? Maybe you're wondering why God would want to do this.

Many times, I read the Bible and encounter what I call an aha! word that explains the who and why behind the what. The aha! word in this passage is "in order" (okay, that's two words). It tells us a key reason why God joined His Son's life with ours (through salvation) to bring us from the dead into new life.

> And God raised us up with Christ and seated us with him in the heavenly realms in Christ Jesus, in order that in the coming ages he might show the incomparable riches of his grace, expressed in his kindness to us in Christ Jesus. (vv. 6–7)

It truly is all about God. On our own, you and I don't have the ability to bring ourselves to life, redeem our past, or forgive our sins. But God does, and He does so for His glory and our good.

3. Express what it means to you to be alive in Christ.

The impact of Jesus's one-time sacrifice is news worth celebrating, and the fact that it's a gift—well, that's just icing on the celebration cake. "For it is by grace you have been saved, through faith—and this is not from yourselves, it is the gift of God" (Eph. 2:8). Because of Jesus, we are alive—no longer the walking dead—and free from the penalty of our sin and the pain of our past.

OVERCOMING THE PAST

Is there something you wish you had never done? Words you'd do anything to take back? For years after truly surrendering my life to this adventure with Christ, the "If Only" song was stuck in my head on auto-play. Over and over the popular chorus, "Woulda, Coulda, Shoulda," boomed in a minor key to unearth buried feelings of regret, reminding me of what I had spent years trying to forget. Maybe you have experienced the same rumble.

I wasn't a bad person. I mean, I didn't do outright unkind things directly in the face of others, but on this side of my younger years, through the lens of redeemed eyes, I clearly see my heart. It was selfish, prideful, critical, and judgmental: a heart unaffected by my actions and unchanged by my salvation. Over time, the Spirit's work in my life led to confession of my past sin, and the grief of my behavior and attitude was replaced with peace and prepared me for the calling on my life.

Don't you know our friend Paul had lots of regrets? The torture, imprisonment, and murder of followers of the God who rescued him from hell had to be painful images for him to carry. Surely, the memory of hearing the screams of the innocent and holding the coats of the murderers haunted Paul. He needed time for the Spirit to teach and train him also.

After Paul's roadside conversion, he spent time in Arabia (Gal. 1:17). Many scholars believe that he used this season (possibly as long as three years) to learn and prepare for public ministry. You see, though Paul's conversion was immediate on the road to Damascus, he still had work to do before he would be ready to step out to preach and teach. Salvation is a miraculous thing, but it doesn't immediately erase the effects of our past.

4. Read 1 Timothy 1:15–16. What did Paul call himself?

5. Did Paul sound defeated or allow his past to keep him from living the immeasurably more life? (See v. 16.) Should we?

6. How did God use Paul's past for his good and God's glory? Is there anything from your past that has kept you from living the immeasurably more life? How could this be used for God's glory?

Without a doubt, who you were before you accepted Christ shapes who you are afterward. Here's the cool thing: God accepts the good, bad, and ugly of our past and creates a beautiful new creation. One of the most encouraging truths in God's Word about getting past our past is 2 Corinthians 5:17. I'm a fan of all Bible translations and love how this verse is rendered in the *Amplified Bible, Classic Edition*. For fun, I included the *New International Version* as well.

> Therefore, if any person is [ingrafted] in Christ (the Messiah) he is a new creation (a new creature altogether); the old [previous moral and spiritual condition] has passed away. Behold, the fresh and new has come! (AMPC)

> Therefore, if anyone is in Christ, the new creation has come: The old has gone, the new is here!

I should have warned you, this news might cause you to spontaneously shout "Hallelujah" or shrill with delight. Take it all in. *The old [previous moral and spiritual condition] is passed away—gone.* We should not waste time remembering what God has forgotten.

Saul determined to be known as *Paul,* his other name, which means "small." He recognized that his experience on the road with Jesus had changed him, and he embraced his status of being a new creation. Below is a New Creation Name Chart. We can shed our past and take hold of our new identity in Christ because of who God is.

New Creation Name Chart

Because God Is	I Am No Longer	I Am
Grace (Eph. 2:8)	Guilty	Forgiven
Just (Rom. 3)	A Failure	Redeemed
Holy (Isa. 1:18; John 1:29)	Shameful	Holy
Merciful (Ps. 145:8)	Cursed	Blessed
Loving (John. 15:16; 1 Peter 2:9)	Unwanted	Chosen
Redeeming (Gal. 4–5)	Guilty	Blameless
Good (Rom. 8:14–17; 1 Peter 1:3)	Abandoned	Adopted
Kind (Titus 3:4–8)	A Beggar	An Heir

Oh, the wondrous love of God, to sacrifice His Son so we might have a new life—a life that's immeasurably more than we could think or ask! "Now to him who is able to do immeasurably more than all we ask or imagine, according to his power that is at work within us" (Eph. 3:20). Jesus did the dying so we might live, so let's cooperate with His Spirit's work so that we might live fully the life He died to give.

We'll close our lesson with a great moving-on verse. It's marked in my Bible to help me remember a significant time in my life when I had to trust God to do a *new thing* in my life, and in the lives of dear friends. He has been faithful to fulfill this verse in immeasurable ways, and I know He will fulfill it for you as well. This one is worth memorizing, highlighting, and hanging on our bathroom mirror.

7. Write out Isaiah 43:18–19 in this space. Then, with your pencil or pen, black out the things we are not supposed to remember or not think about. Circle what God says He is doing.

See you next week, friends! I love doing Bible study with you.

ON YOUR OWN ... IF YOU WANT TO

Go back and look up the verses in our New Creation Name Chart. Ask God to help you add to the chart.

SAY YES TO GOD

Share your Damascus Road experience with someone this week. And if you haven't had one yet, ask a Christian you know to tell you about their story.

Session 2

Yes to God: Nothing Better

PRAYER

Let someone pray for strength to continue walking in obedience.

CONNECT QUESTION

Who is the most obedient person in your family? What makes you think of that person as obedient?

KEY VERSE

"But Samuel replied: 'Does the LORD delight in burnt offerings and sacrifices as much as in obeying the LORD? To obey is better than sacrifice, and to heed is better than the fat of rams'" (1 Sam. 15:22).

BIBLE READING

1 Samuel 15

YNM READING

Chapters 2 and 3

VIDEO LISTENING GUIDE

Obedience does not _____ ____ _____ _____ _____ .

_____ should never come before or after our response to God.

_____ is better than obedience.

Obedience is better than _____ . It's better than our own thinking.

It's better than our own _____ and our own _____ .

We are our own _____ to obedience.

Life with the God of immeasurably more starts when we allow yes to cultivate trust and no to invite revelation, so maybe can welcome freedom.

SESSION 2 NOTES

SESSION 2 DISCUSSION

You've probably seen, or at least heard of, the movie *Chariots of Fire*. (I apologize if the theme song is stuck in your head now!) To recap, the film follows two Olympian runners, one a Jew and one a Christian. The Christ follower is Eric Liddell; it's well known that he changed which leg of the race he ran in order to keep his biblical convictions. But did you know that after he won the gold medal in France, he became a missionary in China? And he died as a prisoner in Japan?[3] It's been reported that he gave up his opportunity to be released so that a pregnant woman could be freed instead.

Here's a man who truly submitted to Jesus as *Kurios* (koo'-ree-os). *Kurios* means "ruler, master, one who exercises authority." Sure, Liddell could have justified bending his convictions in order to ensure winning. And no one would have blamed him if he'd left his missions work in China because of the dangers of Japanese capture. But instead, he made adjustments to his wants and obeyed God without a pause, cause, or clause—just like Paul did on the road to Damascus. (Read more about this amazing moment in Paul's life in chapter 1 in *Yes, No, and Maybe*.) You and I have the same opportunity.

REALIGNING OUR OBEDIENCE

After Paul's conversion and time in Arabia, he taught in Damascus. Yes, Damascus—the very town where he had once headed to persecute Christians before Jesus intervened! It would take courage to visit a town where you had previously set out to rid it of Christians—and to also publicly preach about Christ. Not only would you have to battle your own fear and shame, but you'd also have to face others who knew your history. Back then, religious teachers stood on the temple steps and preached in the open air. Paul would have been front and center before his former Pharisee friends. Can you imagine standing face to face, opposing those to whom you were once aligned? He was different—and now everyone would know.

1. Read Philippians 3:7–10. How did Paul view his life differently after his conversion?

2. How are you different because you are following Christ?

Paul didn't just up and decide one day to boldly proclaim the gospel. Instead, he determined to bravely obey God. He removed the obstacles of self, sin, and shame, and embraced obedience. Paul submitted to Jesus as *Kurios*, and he pursued a lifelong goal of becoming like Him. Jesus pursued Paul, and in return, Paul pursued becoming like Jesus.

> I do not mean that I am already as God wants me to be. I have not yet reached that goal, but I continue trying to reach it and to make it mine. (Phil. 3:12 NCV)

3. What encouragement do you receive from Paul's statements "I have not yet" and "I continue trying"?

Paul went on to say, "Christ wants me to do that, which is the reason he made me his" (v. 12 NCV). The more we know God, the more we love God. The more we love God, the more we want to obey Him as our *Kurios* and do what "Christ wants me to do."

Obedience translates as love to God. It took me a long time to get this. From my vantage point, God and Christianity represented rules to follow. Personally, I didn't like rules at the time and often found ways around them. I mean, what does obedience have to do with love? Great question. Let's get the pages of our Bible moving and connect the dots between obedience and love.

4. Read 1 John 2:5. Who is said to have love for God made complete in them?

5. Read 1 John 5:2–3 and John 14:15. Write out what is defined as or set equal to "love" in these verses.

The message is pretty clear, don't you think? Obedience equals love. God spells *love* like this: o-b-e-y. I'm sure you noticed the use of the verbs *keep* and *obey*. Though different in English, these words translate as the same Greek word, *téreó* (tay-reh'-o). The word means "I keep, guard, observe, watch over."[4] HELPS Word-studies gives us greater insight: "*tēréō* (from tēros, 'a guard')—properly, maintain (preserve); (figuratively) *spiritually guard* (watch) *keep intact.*"[5]

Can we all agree that we love God? Of course we do. If we didn't, we wouldn't be in this Bible study together. That being true, when His Spirit nudges us to take action, what happens to the love? May I suggest that, when presented with the opportunity to obey, we sometimes allow our reasoning to determine our response. In our limited understanding, we offer God a pause, cause, or clause:

- Pause: a delayed response
- Cause: a conditional, "if you do this, I will do that" response
- Clause: a bargaining response

Immediate obedience is the only right response. Proverbs 28:26 uses some strong language about people like me who trust their own thoughts: "A man is a fool to trust himself! But those who use God's wisdom are safe" (TLB). I'm not a fan of that phraseology, but it adequately describes how I behave when I survey my situation and I don't obey. Girls, we have a much better option.

6. Read Proverbs 3:5–6.

Who should we trust?

How should we trust?

What is the result of our trust?

Embrace obedience by trusting God. Say yes, without pause, cause, or clause, and experience a life greater than you could ask for or imagine. Once we enjoy the pleasure of delighting the Lord with our obedience, we will want to remove anything that robs us of the feeling.

REMOVING OUR OBSTACLES

As I mentioned in the book, my son, Griffin, felt the pull of temptation at a young age and knew how to deal with the enticement. His decision wasn't based on parental influence; he felt the nudge of the Spirit. God is always wooing us. He desires to accomplish His goal, to make us holy, as He is holy (1 Peter 1:16). He works through His Spirit and His Word to shape us into His image by helping us remove any obstacles that stand in our way. Ready to obey what He reveals, we rise to overcome the obstacles of self, sin, and shame.

The Obstacle of Self

I don't know about you, but the more time I spend with the God of immeasurably more, the more I realize I am my own worst enemy. I am my biggest obstacle. The Word of God is a "lamp for my feet, a light on my path" (Ps. 119:105), which is so encouraging, right? However, the light also shows all our flaws, as clearly as the picture on HDTV. (Seriously, friends, don't go onscreen without checking for unwanted hairs!) Quite often we just have to get out of the way so God can do His work.

7. Read Psalm 119:59. How does the psalmist advise we view our self?

Taking a hard look at our self through the lens of Scripture isn't easy, but it's the only way to become more like Christ and experience the immeasurably more life. We bid farewell to self and fully embrace our Savior. On occasion self will rise up, but because of His testimonies (His Word and His ways), we can quickly get back into shape. The beauty of self-examination through Scripture prepares us for overcoming the obstacle of sin.

The Obstacle of Sin

It's important to look at the obstacle of sin with this truth: our salvation won't make us not sin, but it will keep us from enjoying it. We are sinners from birth. Hang out with a few toddlers on the playground, and you'll see this is true in a matter of minutes. However, our sin is covered by the blood of Christ. Our part of tackling this obstacle is to do all we can to sin less. And yes, it is possible; it's not always easy, but it is possible.

8. Read Psalm 119:11. How can we sin less? What ways can you devote yourself to this truth?

The Obstacle of Shame

Shame is a painful emotion resulting from an awareness of having done something dishonorable.[6] Can we all agree that no one likes to be made aware of our doing something wrong? It is, well, painful. Our outward response to the inner realization of dishonorable behavior sometimes involves lowering our head.

Maxie reminds me of this every time she doesn't greet me in the driveway. Maxie is my energetic Boykin Spaniel. She loves tennis balls, swimming in the lake, and trying to catch birds—oh, and getting in the trash. Whoever leaves the house last must remember to put the trash can out of her reach. When the "whoever" forgets, Maxie treats herself to a feast. I know she loves every second of ripping that trash bag open and devouring the morsels we scraped from our plates. But when she hears the car pull in the drive, she tucks in her stubby tail, lowers her head, and pitifully pours herself out onto the floor to plead for our forgiveness.

Friends, we need to face Jesus with our sin and confess. But once we receive His forgiveness, we need to walk in freedom, not condemnation. "Therefore, there is now no condemnation for those who are in Christ Jesus" (Rom. 8:1). So if God doesn't condemn us, then why should we condemn ourselves?

When we trust and believe that God has freed us from our sin and shame, we are free to grow in Christlikeness and embrace the immeasurably more life. Paul could have lived in the shadow of his past; it was always before him: "All who heard him were amazed. '*Isn't this* the same man who caused such devastation among Jesus' followers in Jerusalem?' they asked. 'And *didn't he* come here to arrest them and take them in chains to the leading priests?' Saul's preaching became more and more powerful, and the Jews in Damascus couldn't refute his proofs that Jesus was indeed the Messiah" (Acts 9:21–22 NLT).

Our past will often accuse us with these same questions, throwing old sins and shame our way: "Aren't you the one who—? Didn't you once?" But as Christians, our identity is in Christ, not in our past. People couldn't refute Paul's proof that Jesus was the Messiah because of his powerful preaching and because of his profound life change. He shared how we can see a change in ourselves too:

> Forgetting the past and straining toward what is ahead, I keep trying to reach the goal and get the prize for which God called me through Christ to the life above. (Phil. 3:13–14 NCV)

9. Are you more prone to focus on or to forget the past? Why?

10. Read Psalm 3:3. Describe the Lord as the psalmist does.

Oh, let the Lifter of heads place His nail-scarred hands around your beautiful face and whisper, "No more shame. You are a wholly, dearly loved daughter of the Most High King." The more we say yes (submit) to Jesus, the more we are transformed into His image. We'll talk more about this in another lesson, but for now, let's focus on one of God's goals in saving us: "For those God foreknew he also predestined to be *conformed to the image of his Son*" (Rom. 8:29).

See you next week. Bible study is so fun with friends!

ON YOUR OWN ... IF YOU WANT TO

1. Look up Romans 8:1–2. If you have a chance, check out these verses in several different Bible translations. Then on one side of a page, write down all the ways you saw verse 1 say that we have no, or none of, or not something. What is that something? Then on the other side of the page, write down what the Spirit has done for us or given us, according to verse 2.

2. Identify and circle the aha! word or phrase in the following verse. (Here's a helpful hint: the aha! phrase will answer the question "Why does the power of the Spirit free me from sin?")

> And because you belong to him, the power of the
> life-giving Spirit has freed you from the power of
> sin that leads to death. (v. 2 NLT)

3. Find a search-for-a-freedom verse of your own and personalize it as a prayer, thanking God for new life and freedom from the power of self, sin, and shame. Write it out below.

SAY YES TO GOD

Demonstrate your love for God this week by putting these verses into action: "Do nothing out of selfish ambition or vain conceit. Rather, in humility value others above yourselves, not looking to your own interests but each of you to the interests of the others" (Phil 2:3–4). Record what you do and the response you get.

Session 3

No to Self: Reject the Old, Accept the New

PRAYER

Let someone ask God for the courage to reject our old image of ourselves and accept the new image that God has designed for us.

CONNECT QUESTION

Think about what you were like at middle school age. If you could go back and change one thing about yourself then, what would it be?

KEY VERSE

"Those who belong to Christ Jesus have crucified the flesh with its passions and desires" (Gal. 5:24).

BIBLE READING

Galatians 5:13–25

YNM READING

Chapter 4

VIDEO LISTENING GUIDE

Crucifixion of our flesh allows us to

- _____ with Christ Jesus.

- _____ our affections and desires.

- be _____ with the Father.

How can the crucifixion of the flesh happen?

Each day we must make a _____ _____ _____ and yield to the Spirit's work (Gal. 5:25).

Life with the God of immeasurably more starts when we allow yes to cultivate trust and no to invite revelation, so maybe can welcome freedom.

SESSION 3 NOTES

SESSION 3 DISCUSSION

Our word banks are overcrowded with pronouns like *me, mine, my*, and *I*. Our culture feeds self-obsession with Instagram, Facebook, and Twitter. The selfie sensation and LIVE videos have made us all stars of our own world. In today's culture it's commonplace to get rewarded and recognized for every accomplishment, even for accomplishing what is expected.

When my daughter was in elementary school, every year her school had an event called Field Day. Field Day was mandatory for all students, whether they were athletes or not. At the end of the day, everyone received a certificate for participating … in something that what was a *required* activity. Does that make sense?

This kind of culture that offers rewards and attention with very low standards can inflate our ego and further build up an image of *us* in our mind, rather than the One in whose image we were created.

1. Read Genesis 1:27. In whose image were you and I created?

THE IMAGE OF US

Saying we are created in the image of God sounds incredible, but until we truly live like we believe and build our lives on this foundation, these are just words on a page. Often, we dwell on our past, which fuels our unbelief. *How could God have a great plan for a former (fill in blank)? I'm too messed up to be made in the image of God.* It's on this line of thinking that we build the image of us. There are two sides to the "image of us" coin—both are equally destructive to the image of God in us that we should be focusing on: pride and pity.

Pride says this: "All that I have, and all that I am able to accomplish, is due to my hard work, education, and determination." Pity says this: "I will never be able to accomplish anything because I am no good. I am nothing." Both bring attention to us and take away from our devotion to God. As wholly and dearly loved children of God (Col. 3:12), created in the image of God (Gen. 1:27), we have to reject the image of us, and accept the image of God, by the building up of Christ in us.

REJECT CONFORMATION

Rejecting the image of us starts with rejecting the ways of the world's influence. The world wants to change your mind, so it exerts pressure from without. But the Holy Spirit changes your mind by releasing power from within. Warren Wiersbe put it this way: "If the world controls your thinking, you are a conformer; if God controls your thinking, you are a transformer."[7] Let's visit the concept of conformation and then move on to transformation.

Paul loved the people in the churches he had founded. As they held a special place in his heart, he kept in touch with visits and letters as often as he could. When he received word that they weren't following the ways of the culture around them, like a parent or a wise friend, Paul would send loving correction and teaching.

In his letter to the Romans, Paul urged the church to stop putting on their masks and playing like the world. John MacArthur, in his commentary, said the word *conformed* "refers to assuming an outward expression that does not reflect what is really inside, a kind of masquerade or act."[8] I've been guilty of putting on a mask or two in my day. Sometimes it's easier to go along in order to get along, right? However, when we choose to go along with the crowd, we are endorsing their behavior, rather than exalting our Savior.

2. Read Romans 12:1. What mask have you worn, or are you wearing, in order to "get along" with the world?

Rejecting conformation isn't easy. Paul compares it to a living sacrifice. Jews and Gentiles alike would have been familiar with this language. The ceremonial law of that time required a living animal be bound to the altar and offered as a sacrifice to God in order to receive atonement for sin. Have you ever tried to bind the legs of a ram or bull? It might be simpler to herd cats. A sacrifice is the surrender or destruction of something prized or desirable for the sake of something considered as having a higher or more pressing claim.[9] Even though making the offering wasn't easy, it was worth all the effort because what they received in return was atonement. When we offer ourselves to God, we demonstrate that our relationship with Him is more valuable than a relationship with the world.

3. What changes can you make to demonstrate that your relationship with God means more to you than your friendship with the world?

ACCEPT TRANSFORMATION

Just as Paul transformed from a Christian-hater to a Christ-professor, we too can be transformed. In the Greek, the word *transformed* is *metamorphoó* (met-am-or-fo'-o). This one word is comprised of two smaller words (from HELPS Word-studies): "*metá*, '*change after* being *with*' and *morphóō*, 'changing *form* in keeping with inner reality'—properly, transformed *after* being *with*; *transfigured*."[10]

Will you underline the two phrases that begin with the words *change* and *changing* in the previous definition? And for fun, circle the words *inner reality*. I absolutely LOVE the meaning of these two tiny words! For the remainder of the lesson we will break down the how-tos of this change. In order to experience meaningful and lasting transformation, four *T*s must be considered.

Territory

Read Romans 12:2.

4. Where does transformation begin?

5. How does transformation occur?

As David Guzik put it in his *Enduring Word* commentary, "The battle ground between conforming to the world and being transformed is within the mind of the believer."[11] The only way to replace the error of the world's way of thinking is to replace it with God's truth.

Tool

Read Psalm 119:105.

6. What is our tool for transformation?

7. How does it help us?

Even though I was saved at a young age, I didn't really start chasing hard after God until my early thirties, when my happily-ever-after wasn't turning out so happy. I remember confronting two obstacles: lack of resources and lack of training. *Where do I find the answers to my questions about the Bible? How do I understand?* Maybe you've asked the same questions.

We are inundated with resources to help us understand the Bible. There are numerous online Bible commentaries and Bible dictionaries offered for free. Some of my favorite sites are Biblegateway.com and Biblehub.com. These sites introduced me to notable Bible commentators Matthew Henry, Charles Spurgeon, and David Guzik. The market is also flooded with various Bible translations and curricula. Lack of resources is no longer an obstacle. Pick up a Bible and dig in—oh wait, we need a teacher!

Teacher

My parents always told me, "Choose your friends carefully. You become like who you hang out with." Is there a better friend than Jesus? And, girls, when we hang out with Jesus, we change in keeping with our inner reality. Jesus did an awesome thing when He gave His life so that we might have eternal life, but Jesus gave us another gift too.

Read John 16:7.

8. Why did Jesus have to go back to heaven?

Read John 14:26.

9. Who is the Advocate and what is His job?

We are so blessed! The Holy Spirit is our teacher, and He lives inside every believer. "Don't you know that you yourselves are God's temple and that God's Spirit dwells in your midst?" (1 Cor. 3:16). Our teacher is always with us teaching and directing our choices. Isn't this truly amazing? God left the book and sent a teacher! Now, the next *T* is in our hands.

Time

A renewed mind doesn't happen by attending church once a week or randomly participating in a small group Bible study. Don't misunderstand me, exposure to expository teaching through faithful church attendance and Bible study *is* vital to our spiritual growth. However, it's unfair to place the weight of our transformation on the shoulders of our pastors. The greatest victory on the battleground of our mind is experienced through daily study and application of God's Word. (We will talk more about application next week.)

There are no shortcuts or secret formulas to the renewing of our mind, and the renewing of our mind is the pathway to the immeasurably more life.

10. What is the message of Ecclesiastes 3:1–9?

One of my favorite quotes about studying the Bible is from A. W. Tozer (from *That Incredible Christian*): "Whatever keeps me from the Bible is my enemy, however harmless it may appear to be." I know this sounds harsh, but our enemy is real and ruthless. He longs to keep you far from the Word, because the Word is the gateway to the immeasurably more life.

11. What is the "enemy" that keeps you from being wholly devoted to spending time with God each day?

Through knowing our territory and using excellent tools and an excellent teacher, and adding in time, we can know God and His Word and be transformed—we are really without excuse! God's Word—it's a lifesaver as well as a life-giver. Don't miss this life.

ON YOUR OWN ... IF YOU WANT TO

Read Proverbs 13:20: "Become wise by walking with the wise" (THE MESSAGE). The word *walking* means "to advance forward continually."

1. Who do you know who is mature in faith and is already transformed in an area you would like to be transformed in?

How can wise friends play a further part in our transformation? By teaching us with truth and love.

2. Look up Colossians 2:2–3. What do Christians have access to through Christ?

Part of gleaning from wise people is being willing to receive treasure in the form of a reproof, especially when our lives are patterned more after the world than God's Word. If you're anything like me, you don't always enjoy getting slapped on the wrist by Christian friends. It's easier to process when you know that they're wise and speaking in love.

SAY NO TO SELF

This week consider contacting one of the spiritually mature people you know. Talk with that person about helping you stay accountable to being in the Word.

Session 4

No to Self: Godly Training

PRAYER

Let someone ask God for wisdom and endurance as you learn how to enter into godly training.

CONNECT QUESTION

What's one physical exercise that you would like to try?

KEY VERSE

"For physical training is of some value, but godliness has value for all things, holding promise for both the present life and the life to come" (1 Tim. 4:8).

BIBLE READING

1 Timothy 4:7–10

YNM READING

Chapters 5 and 6

VIDEO LISTENING GUIDE

We have to constantly pay attention to our training. Here are some principles for maximizing our godly training.

_____ our trainer.

_____ to the trainer's instructions.

_____ _____ a daily regimen.

_____ to your training.

_____ _____ from false trainers with get-fit-quick plans.

Life with the God of immeasurably more starts when we allow yes to cultivate trust and no to invite revelation, so maybe can welcome freedom.

SESSION 4 NOTES

SESSION 4 DISCUSSION

I'll be the first to admit: I don't like physical training. I admire others who can get up every morning and exercise, and I know I should do it. But I just haven't embraced physical exercise yet. I know more about yogurt (especially frozen) than yoga.

But when it comes to other kinds of training, I'm all in. The structure and regime scratch me right where I itch. I love order. I love clear instructions, the foreknowledge of consequences, and getting results. There truly is freedom in boundaries! I'm not even bothered by a little hard work. Having said all that, I must say this: I prefer the training not be inconvenient or disruptive to my everyday life. Are you nodding your head in a little sisterhood agreement?

Comfortable, convenient training might be possible when learning cooking, crocheting, or other skills, but not when training in the righteousness and selflessness of God's Word. Although the instructions and consequences are clear, godly training is seldom convenient and often does interfere with our daily operations. Let's face it, God's Word is full of love, truth, guidance, and help, but it is also the great divider. In order to assume our new image, we have to allow God's Word to analyze our actions.

1. Read Hebrews 4:12. Write out all the adjectives that describe the Word of God. Write out the verbs that tell what the Word of God does.

Can we agree that some parts of God's Word are harder to process and accept than others? For example, the words *alive* and *active* are hopeful, as well as encouraging. Yet, the rest of the verse is full of words that sound painful, invasive, and unsettling. Unfortunately, we don't get to pick and choose the parts of the Bible we like and will obey. The beautiful thing about God's Word is that the feel-good verses work in harmony with the not-so-feel-good verses. The harmonious blend creates a framework for which the immeasurably more life is built. This life is built on one act of obedience at a time—whether it feels good at the time or not.

The training is where the work of the Spirit and the work of the Word team up to help us assume our new identity in Christ. I remember when the Word first judged my thoughts and attitudes, dividing my soul and spirit. It wasn't pretty.

Read Psalm 141:3. Every report card my parents received concerning my progress in school said the same thing, "Wendy would learn more if she would talk less." Some comments were nicer than others, but generally, the message was simple: my mouth was a huge problem. It makes complete sense that the Lord then started my training with a verse dealing with my mouth. I'm fifty years old and the Spirit (living in me) and the Word (memorized) are still working together to make the words of my mouth pleasing and acceptable in God's sight.

The Spirit discerns and interprets the Scriptures as we study and ingest the Word. With its sharp edges—the hard truths we discover—it works in opposition to the desires of our flesh. The Word is the antidote for the sickness of sin and everything that disguises itself as truth. Submitting to its work, the Spirit will enable us to overcome everything that keeps us from fully enjoying the life Jesus died to give.

In the *Yes, No, and Maybe* book, I talk about three concealers—these are things that can sidetrack our godly training by concealing the image of who God wants us to be. These three culprits have the propensity to sabotage every relationship, especially our relationship with our Savior. By allowing strongholds, self-centeredness, and self-sufficiency to take up real estate in our mind and heart, we can jeopardize the life Jesus died to give: "I came that they may have and enjoy life, and have it in abundance (to the full, till it overflows)" (John 10:10 AMPC). With words like *enjoy, abundance, full,* and *overflow* in our future, it makes sense that we would want to correct these concealers.

STRONGHOLDS

Stronghold is a military term that refers to a fortified or secure place. For a better understanding of its application to life with the immeasurably more God, let's look back at ancient cities. In the Old Testament times, cities were fortified, or walled, for security. Each corner was armed with towers so those on lookout could see trouble coming, warn the guards to close the gates, and prepare for battle. Strongholds protected the city from wicked people coming and prevented wicked people from leaving. Strongholds were powerful.

2. Look up 2 Corinthians 10:4. How does Paul say the weapons we fight with are different from those of the world?

Paul is engaged in a war of words with some in the Corinthian church. Perhaps you've experienced something similar. These are people he loved and mentored, yet they are saying that he is bolder in his letters than he is in person and that he is trying to avoid face-to-face conflict. We see evidence of this in Paul's words: "By the humility and gentleness of Christ, I appeal to you—I, Paul, who am 'timid' when face to face with you, but 'bold' toward you when away!" (2 Cor. 10:1). Basically, some of the Corinthians had been saying that Paul's bark was worse than his bite.

Paul knew what they were saying wasn't true. He had two choices: destroy the falsehoods that were pretending to be true (protect his heart and mind with truth) or let the words move on out (prevent the lie from having power). A stronghold has power, but we have divine power (the Spirit of God living in us) to destroy anything that argues with the truth. "We demolish arguments and every pretension that sets itself up against the knowledge of God, and we take captive every thought to make it obedient to Christ" (v. 5). I absolutely love how HELPS Word-studies breaks down *stronghold*, and you will too!

The Greek word for *stronghold* is *oxýrōma* (okh-oo'-ro-mah), and it is defined as "a heavily-fortified containment" and is said to be, in this verse, "used figuratively of a *false argument* in which a person seeks 'shelter' ('a safe place') to *escape reality*."[12]

3. What is your false shelter? What argument are you hiding behind to stay away from the truth?

4. Read Psalm 9:9 and write the verse below. In what times of trouble has the Lord sheltered you?

King David and Paul leaned on the Lord as their stronghold. We can demolish false arguments and containment systems we have set up with the antidote of truth: "No, in all these things we are more than conquerors through him who loved us" (Rom. 8:37). We can use the divine power of truth to correct the concealers that are keeping us from becoming who God wants us to be.

SELF-CENTEREDNESS

Some words need no explanation. Our next concealer falls into that category. Identifying the problem with self-centeredness is easy: it centers on self, rather than on our Savior. This is why saying no to self can be the hardest discipline to practice. Our flesh fights our spirit, and we have to use the Word to give the death blow to our own desires. The desire to be right, be in charge, and have our own way are outcries from our flesh—they can be loud and steady influences on us. Whew, this is challenging! Without the working and the power of the Spirit, we aren't strong enough to consider others better than us. Yes, I didn't just say consider others *better*.

Paul said it best. In his letter to the Philippian church, Paul encouraged the young church to be one in spirit. He had heard reports of internal conflicts causing the church to be disjointed. So, Paul wrote a perfect prescription for unity in the body. This antidote serves the body of Christ (the church) well, and promotes harmony outside the walls of our churches also. Get ready—this a tough truth to take in.

5. Read Philippians 2:3–4. What is the antidote for the sin of self-centeredness?

6. Move to James 3:16. What is the result of a life that is filled with envy and selfish ambition?

I told you it was a tough truth. The discipline of no to self is where we demonstrate how serious we are about having an intimate relationship with Christ. Putting others first is taking on the nature of Christ. Later in Philippians 2, Paul said:

> Your attitude should be the kind that was shown us by Jesus Christ, who, though he was God, did not demand and cling to his rights as God, but laid aside his mighty power and glory, taking the disguise of a slave and becoming like men. And he humbled himself even further, going so far as actually to die a criminal's death on a cross. (vv. 5–8 TLB)

It is unlikely you or I will ever be subject to a criminal's death on a cross. However, Jesus likens our dying to self as a sacrificial death. He makes it very clear that to be a disciple, we must be willing to lay down our rights each day. "Then Jesus said to his disciples, 'If any of you wants to be my follower, you must give up your own way, take up your cross, and follow me'" (Matt. 16:24 NLT). This life is not about us; it's all about Jesus. When we get this, truth takes root in our heart, and the immeasurably more life is but a stone's throw away.

SELF-SUFFICIENCY

We are taught from a very young age to be independent. Our parents celebrated when we could walk, feed ourselves, and learn to ride our bikes without training wheels. These are just a few of the self-sufficient milestones that show we are growing and learning. While education and independence are good things, demonstrating responsibility and maturity are equally significant. The danger of higher education and personal achievement is that they often invite the final concealer, self-sufficiency, to gain power in our lives and get in the way of our relationship with the God of immeasurably more.

Humans were created in the likeness of God to live in fellowship with God. Living in relationship with someone creates a dependency on that person—you develop trust. For over twenty-five years I have lived in a married relationship with my husband, Scott. We've learned to depend on and trust each other. The same is true in our love relationship with God, Jesus, and the Holy Spirit (the Trinity). Rather than marvel at our self-sufficiency, let's live the marvel of God-sufficiency.

As important as the apostle Paul was to the early church, he never rode into town on his own coattails. There were false teachers and prophets running rampant in the time of the early church. Therefore, it was commonplace when communicating with churches, both personally and through letters, to verify your credentials. In confirming his identification in his second letter to the church at Corinth, Paul was quick to acknowledge where acknowledgement was due.

> We dare to say these good things about ourselves only because of our great trust in God through Christ, that he will help us to be true to what we say, and not because we think we can do anything of lasting value by ourselves. Our only power and success comes from God. (2 Cor. 3:4–5 TLB)

7. In what ways do you rely on yourself rather than God?

The no to self training is truly transforming. It's not easy to look at yourself in the light of Scripture, but all the seed sowing and cultivating of the Word is worth the harvest: a likeness to Christ. When we start to look like Christ and act like Christ, the world around us notices. A freedom like nothing this world can offer floods our soul as we become sold out to the cause and kingdom of Christ. Train hard, my friend … train hard.

See you next week. Let's stay in the Word.

ON YOUR OWN ... IF YOU WANT TO

Read 2 Timothy 3:16–17 and think about the four terms listed below. Underneath the list, write out specific benefits you have received from reading God's Word that fall into any of these four categories. Or, if you are new to reading the Bible, write out what you hope to achieve or goals you'd like to reach in your life through studying God's Word.

- *Teaching:* giving instruction
- *Reproof:* reproachment or conviction
- *Correction:* restoration to the proper condition
- *Training:* instructing someone to reach maturity

SAY NO TO SELF

Identify your concealer (strongholds, self-centeredness, self-sufficiency). Use Biblegateway.com or another Bible resource to locate verses that will help you correct it. Write the verses on a piece of paper and repeat them out loud when you are faced with a struggle.

Session 5

Maybe Welcomes Freedom: Living Confidently for Christ

PRAYER

Let someone pray and thank God for the freedom we have in Christ.

CONNECT QUESTION

Identify at least two people who fit into these categories (one person per category): has been caught in a trap, and has freed someone or something from a trap. Share each other's stories.

KEY VERSE

"Now the Lord is the Spirit, and where the Spirit of the Lord is, there is freedom" (2 Cor. 3:17).

BIBLE READING

2 Corinthians 3:7–18

YNM READING

Chapter 7

VIDEO LISTENING GUIDE

We have freedom *for* the

- _____ living of His
  Word—not under the condemnation of the Law.

- _____ of
  the kingdom of God—not our own agenda.

- _____ of His
  glory—not our own.

And we have freedom *from* _____ , so
that we can live *for* Him.

**Life with the God of immeasurably more starts when we allow
yes to cultivate trust and no to invite revelation, so maybe can
welcome freedom.**

SESSION 5 NOTES

SESSION 5 DISCUSSION

Living by the disciplines of yes to God and no to self not only builds a trust relationship with the Lord, it provides a firm foundation for maybe. As we continue to live by the Word and allow the Spirit to work in us, we develop spiritual strength and are empowered to overcome our flesh. This ignites a celebratory spirit for all Christ has done for us, and all He has done in us.

Our new image becomes second nature, and our spirit is overtaken with an awareness of a freedom we've never known, but always longed to experience. We recognize and celebrate our freedom *from* the image of our life before Christ, *from* the pull sin has on our life, and *from* plans we permitted our past to dictate for our life. Freedom *from* the flesh invites us to live in freedom *for* the kingdom of God.

1. Read Galatians 5:1. What is compared to the burden of *not* living in the freedom that Christ came to give?

Contextually Paul was addressing a falsehood being taught in the church: the church needed to obey the law (given by Moses), as well as be saved through faith in Jesus. However, without compromising the integrity of Scripture, we can make a connection to our invitation to freedom.

Circle the words *burden* and *slavery* and let's have a quick vocabulary lesson. *Burden* as a verb means "to load someone down—to put some kind of heaviness on someone, whether a physical weight or a mental or spiritual one." *Slavery* means "being in bondage," which implies involuntary servitude. It's the condition in which someone is bound and forced to submit to another's control.[13] What we say yes *to* has power *over* us. This is why it is crucial to live fully in the liberty that Christ died to give us and say yes to His instructions. When we embrace our freedom and live *for* the Freedom Giver, we are less likely to be shackled to sin and the seductions of the world.

The most common use of the word *yoke* is to describe the large device that binds two oxen together for the purpose of plowing. However, Dictionary.com offers several other suggestions that make the word very intriguing: "an agency of oppression, subjection, servitude, etc." and "something that couples or binds together, a bond." Paul uses *yoke* as a term of servitude, warning us against the power of sin and its effect on our freedom in Christ. Paul is not the only person in the Bible to speak of a yoke. Let's turn back in our Bibles to the first gospel.

2. Read Matthew 11:29–30. Who is speaking? How is His definition of yoke different from Paul's?

Rather than being bound by iniquity, Jesus suggests we can bind ourselves to Him for a life that is light, easy, and full of learning. God's yoke is not burdensome; it's easy to bear (light), meaning that it's useful, mild, pleasant, and benevolent.[14] *The Message* version of these verses offer another way to envision this kind of partnership that Jesus is speaking of:

> Are you tired? Worn out? Burned out on religion? Come to me. Get away with me and you'll recover your life. I'll show you how to take a real rest. Walk with me and work with me—watch how I do it. Learn the unforced rhythms of grace. I won't lay anything heavy or ill-fitting on you. Keep company with me and you'll learn to live freely and lightly. (vv. 28–30)

God freed us *from* a life yoked to the world and its pleasures *for* a life yoked with Him, to love and serve the world in His name. The fresh air of freedom flows through our veins as maybe welcomes the freedom *for* radical living, lavish loving, and generous giving.

RADICAL LIVING

Radical is a word that often puts people on high alert, because its very definition suggests favoring something other than the status quo. Most of us would fear someone who lived life in opposition of existing views, habits, and conditions. Our friend Paul lived his life on the far side of extreme, both before his encounter with Jesus and after. Before his Damascus Road experience, he set out to capture and kill Christians. After he was blinded by the light of Jesus, Paul began to preach the very gospel that he had killed others for believing. I think we can all agree Paul was a radical of his day.

When we respond to God with complete obedience, the pull to radical living, living counter to our culture, can't be ignored. Listen to how Paul explained his encounter with Jesus to King Agrippa after being arrested and imprisoned for teaching the radical and extreme message of being made right with God through Jesus rather than the Law.

> What could I do, King Agrippa? I couldn't just walk away from a vision like that! I became an obedient believer on the spot. I started preaching this life-change—this radical turn to God and everything it meant in everyday life—right there in Damascus, went on to Jerusalem and the surrounding countryside, and from there to the whole world. (Acts 26:19–20 THE MESSAGE)

His turn to God was instant and unwavering. Oh, how I wish I could say the same about my conversion to Christianity. My move to radical living was slow going. I was in my early thirties when I finally decided to relinquish control of my life, allowing Him to truly be my Lord, not just my Savior. Until then, I was just a pew warmer, living for myself every day except Sunday. Not Paul. From the moment he met Jesus on the road, until the day he met Him in heaven, Paul lived out the greatest calling—the calling all Christians have on our lives—with complete abandon.

Radical living can be defined as living in a way to produce real change to practices and conditions present in society. This perfectly describes Jesus and Paul. Everything they taught and did was counter to the culture in which they lived. I love the way Paul, in Philippians 2:5–8, discussed the radical choices Jesus made when He came to earth:

You must have the same attitude that Christ Jesus had.

Though he was God,
    he did not think of equality with God
    as something to cling to.
Instead, he gave up his divine privileges;
    he took the humble position of a slave
    and was born as a human being.
When he appeared in human form,
    he humbled himself in obedience to God
    and died a criminal's death on a cross. (NLT)

Paul clearly outlines the way of radical living. He challenges us to think the way Jesus thought. WOW! What a concept! Underline the phrases of radical living. *He gave up his privileges. He took the humble position of a slave. He humbled himself in obedience to God.* Jesus didn't cling to anything, He willingly served everyone, and He humbly obeyed God.

3. Examine Paul's radical-living phrases. What part of radical living is most challenging to you?

Radical living is a lifestyle change for most of us. It's only possible by the indwelling of the Holy Spirit. He enables us to surrender, serve, and see others as more important than ourselves. Accepting the invitation of freedom *for* surpasses any life we can ever ask or imagine, and radical living is just the beginning.

LAVISH LOVING

Another beautiful freedom *for* is lavish loving. With all transparency and an honest examination of myself, I'd like to think I'm a nice person—kind to others in a general way. However, the more I've allowed yes to cultivate trust and no to invite revelation, my heart response to the needs and cries of others has quickened. God has provided countless opportunities for me to demonstrate His love to others.

In recent months, He has challenged me to "Notice them"—those individuals who are often overlooked, specifically the unthanked people who slide my items for purchase over the electric scanner, serve my food over the counter, and smile at me through the teller window at the bank. "Call them by name," God whispered to my spirit. At first it was awkward. Now, well, it is part of my checkout process.

It's so simple: show love. Paul refers to this love as part of the freedom we are to enjoy as children of God. Read his words in Galatians 5:13–14:

> You, my brothers and sisters, were called to be free.
> But do not use your freedom to indulge the flesh;
> rather, serve one another humbly in love. For the
> entire law is fulfilled in keeping this one command:
> "Love your neighbor as yourself."

4. Read John 13:35. How will others know we are Jesus's disciples? In what ways are you currently demonstrating that you are a disciple of Jesus?

If we're honest, not everyone is easy to love. As much as we may want to, we don't get to create a "Love" list and a "Don't Love" list.

But lavish loving will transform us in ways that will astound. It supplies the capacity to forgive those who have hurt us and the power to pray for our enemies. In freedom *for* lavish loving, love no longer feels like a command that Jesus gave, but a gift we are privileged to give. We have love to give and so much more.

GENEROUS GIVING

When I was little, my church supplied every member with giving envelopes. My parents taught me all about tithing a tenth of my income (even when I only made $2.25 in babysitting money). They also taught me to give to special offerings and needs. I grew to love placing my offering in the plate, as the deacons passed it each Sunday. As awesome as tithing and placing a gift of love in the offering plate might be, giving is not all about money. If we make giving synonymous with money, most of us would never give, because most of us don't have a lot of money. Giving is a gift from God—money is just one thing we have the opportunity to give.

5. Read Romans 12:6–8. Name the gifts God generously gives.

Something happens when we live the immeasurably more life with our immeasurably more God: the liberty in our living motivates us to release the grip on our time, talents, tithes, and treasures. Joyfully, we abandon our *T*s for the furthering of God's kingdom. We realize that everything we have was created by and belongs to Him; therefore, we are compelled to work with joy for the furthering of God's plan. "God is the One who made all things, and all things are for his glory" (Heb. 2:10 NCV). Generous giving and pleasing our heavenly Father become a natural way of life.

6. How would you define or describe your giving?

Paul spent his life living radically, loving lavishly, and giving generously. His missionary journeys resulted in the movement of the Christian faith among Gentiles. Even from within the walls of prison, he encouraged those on the journey with Christ, mentored young leaders, and witnessed to those who held him captive. Even when confined, Paul was free. This is the freedom the immeasurably more life generates, friends. Let's grab it and never let go!

See you next week. Let's stay in the Word.

ON YOUR OWN ... IF YOU WANT TO

If you have the *Yes, No, and Maybe* book, take the Spiritual Gifts Assessment provided in the back to discover your areas of giftedness. Begin to pray how God would have you use your gifts for His glory. (If you don't have the book, you can take other spiritual gifts evaluations online.)

SAY MAYBE TO FREEDOM

Choose one to demonstrate this week: radical living, lavish loving, or generous giving. Write about your experience.

Session 6

Maybe: Considering, Confirming, and Completing

PRAYER

Pray together, asking God for the passion and energy to finish well.

CONNECT QUESTION

Have you ever had the experience of crossing a finish line? What was that like?

KEY VERSE

"However, I consider my life worth nothing to me; my only aim is to finish the race and complete the task the Lord Jesus has given me—the task of testifying to the good news of God's grace." (Acts 20:24)

BIBLE READING

Acts 20:20–30

YNM READING

Chapters 8 and 9

VIDEO LISTENING GUIDE

Finishing well

- _____ nothing—it leaves nothing to chance.

- _____ the Spirit's leading.

- _____ with joy—no matter what the circumstances.

Life with the God of immeasurably more starts when we allow yes to cultivate trust and no to invite revelation, so maybe can welcome freedom.

SESSION 6 NOTES

SESSION 6 DISCUSSION

My parents had me later in their married life, therefore, I grew up around older children and adults. When you are surrounded by grown-ups, you start to feel like you are a grown-up, and should have privileges associated with being older: a later bedtime, money to buy stuff, and an open-door coming-and-going policy. You can imagine the frustration this caused me, not to mention the anxiety my parents must have experienced. In order to keep me in line, I heard the word *maybe* often. Oh, how it frustrated me! Perhaps this is why *maybe used to be* one of my least favorite words.

Maybe is defined as neither yes or no. It's a modifier, which means the word has the power to qualify a phrase or action. *Maybe* presses pause, offering freedom from giving a definite answer until an informed and appropriate response is reached. Let's just say, I no longer detest the word—I embrace it. In using *maybe* as a response, we are exercising freedom and honoring God by making good decisions, using our good gifts for the good service He created for us.

1. Discuss a time that you have used the response "Maybe" as a way of putting someone off, or when you really meant "No." And talk about times you've said "Maybe" and honestly meant that you would give the situation some thought.

Maybe, the modifier, welcomes spiritual freedom, but it is sometimes misunderstood. It can be translated as "I'm saying maybe to buy some time until I have the gumption to say no." It's similar to when we say, "Oh, wow, thanks for asking. Let me pray about it," when we have no intention of praying, because we don't want the assignment. Sadly, there have been times I've offered up a "Maybe" in both of these ways. Perhaps worse, there have been times when I've said "Yes," but I knew that "No" was the best answer.

How can an eager-to-serve, Jesus-loving, immeasurably-more-living girl be certain of her God-given assignments? She can be certain when she confirms and considers.

CONFIRM WITH CONFIDENCE

If I had to, I would guess that "How do I know it's God speaking?" is one of the most asked questions by Christians. Much to our dismay, there is not a test to confirm God's voice. As much as we'd like for God to send us an instant message, email, or text message, the only way to confirm God's voice is to learn to recognize it; it's that simple and that complex. In the Old Testament God spoke through prophets like Samuel, Joel, and Ezra. Today, He communicates with His children through His Holy Spirit with His Word and prayer.

2. How is God communicating in the following circumstances?

Exodus 3:4

Exodus 24:16

Numbers 22:26–28

3. How is God's voice described in the following scriptures?

Job 37:4

1 Samuel 2:10

While I have not experienced any of the above—although a talking donkey would be very interesting, as well as entertaining—I've gained confidence in recognizing the way God communicates. Notice I said *gained* confidence—I'm not completely confident. Understanding God, His ways, and His instructions is refined by a daily commitment to study His Word and a fervent prayer life. Recognizing God's communication is enhanced by the maturity of our faith and our willingness to obey. God speaks however He chooses; and I've found He speaks through repetition, requests to move, and reaffirmation.

Repetition

I grew up in the '80s: the years of big hair, disco pants, cassette tapes, and rock music. Occasionally, I relive the glory days and turn my radio to the oldies station. Decades later I can belt out every word of familiar songs. How? I invested time in learning the words and listened repeatedly. The same philosophy is true when it comes to hearing and understanding God.

The result of time invested in prayer and studying the Bible is knowing and hearing God. We repeat our investment on a daily basis, and God repeats His instructions to ensure understanding. Have you been in church, listening to the radio, or speaking to a friend only to hear the same scripture or general message? That's God, my friend—not coincidence, but God. He speaks through repetition. I love that about Him, because I am slow and don't always get the message the first time. Can I get a witness?

4. Read John 10:1–18. Who are the sheep? Who is the shepherd?

5. In John 10:4, what action do the sheep take and why?

Sheep spend a lot of time with their shepherd. They follow him because they are used to being with him. They are well practiced in following the shepherd. They know his voice. His commands are a familiar sound to them. They know what words he uses, and with just a little prodding, they can tell where he wants them to go. The more time we spend with God, the more we can know Him. As we get to know Him, we will be confident in knowing His voice, which is essential when He requests a move.

Requests to Move

Although God does often ask us to move physically, I'm referring here to a different kind of move—the zone move. When God wants to challenge us and make us grow, He seems to be concerned very little with our contentment or comfort. He often moves us from the comfort zone to the conformation zone. God desires us to conform to His ways and His plan. This, more often than not, is in great conflict with our plan. When you sense that you are being pulled out of your comfort zone, especially when it comes to service to the kingdom of God, more than likely God is speaking to you.

6. Read Acts 20:21–23. How did Paul determine where to go? In what way could this decision have been uncomfortable for Paul?

Paul often returned to places where he had been previously mistreated. Although many missionaries around the world suffer, and have even died because of their obedience to Christ, it's not likely that you or I will face physical dangers such as being stoned or receiving death threats. But we may have to face our own personal fears. We may be asked to start a Bible study in our neighborhood, begin a new ministry at church, or quit our job for full-time ministry.

There's no doubt about it, moving out of our comfort zone to accept an assignment to serve, wherever that may be, can be scary. However, we can walk in the certainty that it's possible to be content in the uncomfortable because God called us to it, and He will see us through it. And because He loves us so, He repeats and reaffirms His instructions.

Reaffirmation

The word *affirmation* means to confirm the truth. God speaks through reaffirmation to affirm what He has said. He not only uses His Word, but He also uses His people.

My call to ministry was out of my comfort zone, and I kept it between me and God for a while. He repeated His message through the spiritual gifts assessment I completed. Numerous places in Scripture pointed me to individuals who moved from their comfort zone to accept God's calling: Abraham, Jonah, and Esther—just to name a few. And even though I had become fairly certain about my calling, God was sweet enough to send a message of reaffirmation.

Marilyn was our church's receptionist, but quickly became a trusted friend. While in the church office, she approached me. "Wendy," she said, "I have verse for you." She opened her Bible to show me 1 Peter 4:11, "Do you have the gift of speaking? Then speak as though God himself were speaking through you" (NLT). It's been more than fifteen years, and my knees still feel weak as I recall the moment. Trembling inside and out, I fumbled to find the words to share my calling to speak. God is so faithful to confirm Himself to us.

There is so much more that can be said on this subject, but we'll table it for another study. The bottom line is: God speaks to His children, all of His children, not just the preachers, Bible teachers, and those in Christian leadership. *You* can confidently confirm God's voice and then spend time with Him as you freely consider ministry and service assignments.

7. How have you seen experienced repetition, requests to move, and reaffirmation in your life?

CONSIDER WITH FREEDOM

Recognizing God's voice is the foundation for making the right commitments to serve. Standing on the firm footing of this confidence, it's time to consider. Dictionary.com tells us that *consider* means "to think carefully and contemplate in order to make a decision." We carefully think about a lot of important things: who and if we will marry, which job opportunity is best, where we will go on vacation, and how we will budget our money. But do we truly and thoroughly consider how we can serve God and advance His kingdom?

Considering helps us avoid overcommitment and neglecting our responsibilities, and it helps us ensure that we are selecting the right assignments. Oswald Chambers said it best:

> Our ordinary and reasonable service to God may actually compete against our total surrender to Him. Our reasonable work is based on the following argument which we say to ourselves, "Remember how useful you are here, and think how much value you would be in that particular type of work." That attitude chooses our own judgment, instead of Jesus Christ, to be our guide as to where we should go and where we could be used the most. Never consider whether or not you are of use—but always consider that "you are not your own" (1 Corinthians 6:19). You are His.[15]

When living in the freedom of maybe, we joyously offer our time, talents, tithe, and treasures to be used for God's glory, while also taking the time necessary to accept the assignments that are best suited for us and complement our life. Ministry, even assignments outside our comfort zone, will overall complement, rather than complicate, our life. Accepting the right assignment at the right time is essential to avoid ministry burnout and service overload. With godly confidence, it's best to qualify (consider) each opportunity to serve with the freedom of maybe.

I've compiled a Consider Checklist to contemplate before committing. It's such a blessing to be in the place of *freedom*—the place where we know God's voice and live to please Him and only Him. Paul, though in prison, lived in this freedom. "Obviously, I'm not trying to win the approval of people, but of God. If pleasing people were my goal, I would not be Christ's servant" (Gal. 1:10 NLT).

Consider Checklist

Consider Your ...	By Asking Good Questions
People	Who depends on me for the basic necessities of life? How often am I needed in order to provide such care? What are my significant other's thoughts about my decision? How does my family feel about my making this commitment?

Commitments	To what else am I committed?
	How often will I be needed (daily, weekly, biweekly)?
	What is required of me?
Gifts	Will I be working within my area of giftedness?
	Have I completed a spiritual gifts assessment?
	How will my gifts be used?
Zone	Is this in my comfort zone or is God stretching me?
Enemy	What obstacles have been set before me?
	Have I claimed victory in the decision and told Satan to flee?
	Have I invited others to pray for me?
Confirmation	How has God confirmed a yes or a no?
	What has been repeated and reaffirmed?

8. Where do you fall short in your considering? Where are you strong in considering?

9. What can you do to become better at considering?

Lastly, considering must be covered in prayer. Prayer is where confirmation, as well as reaffirmation, come. It is through prayer that God communicates all we need to know about the decision. He equips us for the adventure of yes, gives us courage to say no, and continues to fellowship with us through the freedom of immeasurably more living.

ALL THIS COMES WITH A WARNING

The spiritual freedom that *maybe*, the modifier, welcomes is captivating. It creates excitement in us for Christ and His kingdom—a longing to exert ourselves serving, studying His Word, and saying yes to whatever He asks to take over our flesh. All of these are good things. However, unless we learn the power of maybe, our exertion can turn to exhaustion, and exhaustion leads to spiritual fatigue. What we say yes to has power over us, which can make service feel more like an obligatory oppression than a blessed opportunity. The freedom flame can flicker and sputter and finally burn out.

Cultivating trust and inviting revelation lay the groundwork for living in the freedom that maybe welcomes. It is in this freedom real peace in our relationship is found. This is the peace that Jesus—fully God, yet fully man—experienced when He cried out in the garden of Gethsemane, "Father, if you are willing, please take this cup of suffering away from me. Yet I want your will to be done, not mine" (Luke 22:42 NLT). Paul experienced this peace while living in a Roman prison and wrote, "For to me, to live is Christ and to die is gain" (Phil. 1:21).

This peace, this freedom, this immeasurably more life with our immeasurably more God is waiting for you. It's a life worth every yes we utter, every revelation we humbly align with His truth, and every act of service we consider. He is worthy.

I want to finish up this session and send you out with this prayer from Paul's words:

> So I bow in prayer before the Father from whom every family in heaven and on earth gets its true name. I ask the Father in his great glory to give you the power to be strong inwardly through his Spirit. I pray that Christ will live in your hearts by faith and that your life will be strong in love and be built on love. And I pray that you and all God's holy people will have the power to understand the greatness of Christ's love—how wide and how long and how high and how deep that love is. Christ's love is greater than anyone can ever know, but I pray that

you will be able to know that love. Then you can be filled with the fullness of God.

With God's power working in us, God can do much, much more than anything we can ask or imagine. To him be glory in the church and in Christ Jesus for all time, forever and ever. Amen. (Eph. 3:14–21 NCV)

Cultivate trust with yes.
Invite revelation with no.
Welcome freedom with maybe.

ON YOUR OWN ... IF YOU WANT TO

Read Philippians 1:3–6. In these verses Paul was giving thanks for the Philippians for being partners with him (and with Timothy) in gospel work. He was "confident" that God—the One who had begun the good work within them—would stay with them and help bring that work to its completion, until the "day of Christ Jesus."

What gospel work have you started but left unfinished? Or what have you not even started yet? Maybe there's a relationship that you've let slide, or an apology that ought to be given, and you haven't worked up the will to do it yet. Or maybe you've had a nudging from God for a while to participate in a part of ministry, or to talk to someone about Jesus, or to reach out to someone to ask how you can help, and you've been trying to ignore that providential poking in your side. Do two things this week:

1. Identify your unfinished piece of gospel work.

2. Take one step toward completing that task.

God has begun a good work in you—He's not going to let you fail in that work. You can take a step toward the finish line with complete confidence that He will be with you every inch of the way!

SAY MAYBE TO FREEDOM

Now that you've gone through this study, consider who else might benefit from knowing the things you've learned here. Maybe there are even people in your neighborhood who are feeling stuck in their lives and not so sure where to go for help. Maybe there are women in a shelter or in a hospital or even in prison who could benefit from learning about the Yes, No, and Maybe adventure. You don't have to be an expert Bible teacher to use this guide to help someone learn more about what life with the God of immeasurably more can be like. Think about who might need to hear what you've learned, and consider sharing your story with someone this week or in the very near future.

Bonus Session

One More Conversation

DISCUSSION

As you finish up your study time together, you may want to gather with your group one last time to share your thoughts about what you've discovered along the way, to swap stories, and to dream about what life with the God of immeasurably more might hold for you. A conversation with two dear people in my life is included in the *Yes, No, and Maybe Video Series* to encourage you and to inspire you to take steps to begin your Yes, No, and Maybe adventure with God right now.

1. If you have watched this conversation between my friends, Lauren and Linda, and me, what stood out to you about these stories?

2. How did each of us say yes, no, or maybe in our situations?

3. Revisit Philippians 2:3. What does this verse say not to be? What does it say to be?

4. How can knowing a verse like this help us in our Yes, No, and Maybe adventure?

5. Read Proverbs 15:31. What did I say I did or didn't like about this verse?

6. How did Linda's yes to God help me say no to self?

Here are some things to remember about the steps you can take to begin your journey with the God of immeasurably more:

- They don't have to be big steps.
- They may not even look like steps at first.

- Opportunities to take them may pop up at the most unexpected times and through the most unlikely people.

If you need help remembering what some of these steps are, here's a quick refresher:

- Saying yes to God means yielding to His will, His teachings, and His righteousness.
- Saying yes to God means obeying what He says in His Word. Nothing is better than that!
- Saying no to our old self means sacrificing the passions and desires of our flesh.
- Saying no to self requires training for godliness— every day!
- Saying maybe allows us to walk out God's Word freely and with confidence—living radically, loving lavishly, and giving generously.
- Saying maybe encourages and equips us to finish well. Whatever the task is that God has given us, we can finish it well.

And if that list is still too long for you, here's the super-simple steps:

1. Open God's Word every day.
2. Read it.
3. Talk to God about it.

If you just do those three things every day, you will be amazed at the changes God will bring to your heart, soul, and mind. I'm so blessed to have been able to join you at the very start of your journey toward the life God created you to have. Let's keep the conversation going! Please join me on my Facebook page or on my website, www.wendypope.org. I can't wait to see you there!

Notes

1. HELPS Word-studies, s.v. "*sýn*," Bible Hub, accessed July 27, 2018, http://biblehub.com/greek/4862.htm.

2. HELPS Word-studies, s.v. "*zōopoiéō*," Bible Hub, accessed July 27, 2018, http://biblehub.com/greek/2227.htm.

3. "A Short Biography of Eric H. Liddell," Eric Liddell Centre, accessed July 27, 2018, www.ericliddell.org/about-us/eric-liddell/biography/.

4. Dodson Dictionary, s.v. "*téreó*," GreekLexicon.org, accessed July 27, 2018, http://greeklexicon.org/lexicon/strongs/5083/.

5. HELPS Word-studies, s.v. "*tēréō*," GreekLexicon.org, accessed July 27, 2018, http://greeklexicon.org/lexicon/strongs/5083/.

6. Dictionary.com, s.v. "shame," accessed July 27, 2018, www.dictionary.com/browse/shame?s=t.

7. Warren W. Wiersbe, *The Wiersbe Bible Commentary NT* (Colorado Springs: David C Cook, 2007), 442.

8. John MacArthur, *The MacArthur Study Bible (ESV)* (Wheaton, IL: Crossway, 2017), 1671–72.

9. Dictionary.com, s.v. "sacrifice," accessed August 1, 2018, www.dictionary.com/browse/sacrifice.

10. HELPS Word-studies, s.v. "*metamorphóō*," Bible Hub, accessed July 27, 2018, http://biblehub.com/greek/3339.htm.

11. David Guzik, "Romans 12—Living the Christian Life," in *The Enduring Word Bible Commentary*, accessed July 27, 2018, https://enduringword.com/bible-commentary/romans-12/.

12. HELPS Word-studies, s.v. "*oxýrōma*," Bible Hub, accessed July 27, 2018, http://biblehub.com/greek/3794.htm.

13. Dictionary.com, s.v. "bondage," accessed July 27, 2018, www.dictionary.com/browse/bondage?s=t.

14. Strong's Concordance, s.v. "*chrēstós*," StudyLight.org, accessed July 27, 2018, www.studylight.org/lexicons/greek/5543.html.

15. "My Utmost—March," My Utmost for His Highest, accessed July 27, 2018, https://utmost.org/march.

About the Author

Wendy is the wife of Scott, mother of Blaire and Griffin, author, speaker, and Bible study teacher. She loves lazy Sundays watching golf with her husband, thrift-store shopping with her daughter, and watching building shows with her son.

Wendy is the author of *Wait and See: Finding Peace in God's Pauses and Plans and the Wait and See Participant's Guide: A Six-Session Study on Waiting Well.* She is a contributing author to the *Real-Life Women's Devotional Bible, Encouragement for Today: Devotions for Daily Living, The Reason We Speak,* and *God's Purpose for Every Woman.*

She leads women all over the world to life change through her in-depth online Bible studies. Down-to-earth and transparent, Wendy teaches in a way that women feel she is speaking directly to their hearts. She has led thousands of women through her Read Thru the Word (RTW) study of the *One Year Chronological Bible.* To grow your faith and passion for God's Word, see information about Wendy's RTW class at wendypope.org/online-studies.

Her messages are filled with biblical insights but sprinkled with just the right amount of humor to help her audiences see she is a real, everyday woman. Wendy inspires her audiences to:

- make spending time in God's Word each day a priority.
- look for God working around them every day.
- view life with a God-first perspective.

To bring the message of *Yes, No, and Maybe* or another of Wendy's inspiring topics to your next event, contact speakercoordinator @proverbs31.org.

CONNECT WITH WENDY

Website: wendypope.org
Email: wendy@wendypope.org
Facebook: www.facebook.com/WendyPopeOfficial
Twitter: @wendybpope
Instagram: Wendy_Pope
Pinterest: www.pinterest.com/wendypope67

Proverbs 31
MINISTRIES

ABOUT PROVERBS 31 MINISTRIES

If you were inspired by the *Yes, No, and Maybe Study Guide* and desire to deepen your own personal relationship with Jesus Christ, I encourage you to connect with Proverbs 31 Ministries.

Proverbs 31 Ministries exists to be a trusted friend who will take you by the hand and walk by your side, leading you one step closer to the heart of God through:

- Free online daily devotions
- First 5 Bible study app
- Daily radio program
- Books and resources
- Online Bible studies
- COMPEL writers training, www.CompelTraining.com

To learn more about Proverbs 31 Ministries, call 877-731-4663 or visit www.Proverbs31.org.

Proverbs 31 Ministries
630 Team Rd., Suite 100
Matthews, NC 28105
www.Proverbs31.org

Bible Credits